I'm Through!
What Can I Do?

Written by Linda Schwartz
Illustrated by Kathy Parks

The Learning Works, Inc.

The Learning Works

Editor: Kimberley Clark
Illustrator: Kathy Parks
Book Design: Clark Editorial & Design
Cover Illustrator: Karl Edwards
Cover Designer: Barbara Peterson
Project Director: Linda Schwartz

Reprinted ©2007
Copyright © 2002
The Learning Works, Inc.

Contents

To the Teacher 5

═══════════ **Fun with Words** ═══════════

Mystery Message #1 6
Mystery Message #2 7
Mystery Message #3 8
Mystery Message #4 9
Ferris Wheel Fun 10
Flower Power 11
Letter Links 12
More Letter Links 13
Homophone Crossword Puzzle 14
Synonym Crossword Puzzle 15
Antonym Crossword Puzzle 16
Hide Four 17
Noun Packages 18

═══════ **Number and Shape Puzzles** ═══════

Circus Sums 19
Find Four Foxes 20
Magic Square 21
Number Search Puzzle #1 22
Number Search Puzzle #2 23
Pattern Puzzle #1 24
Pattern Puzzle #2 25
Addition Magician 26
Subtraction Submarine 27
Multiplication Monkey 28
Division Dive 29
Farmer Frank 30
Switch-a-Roo 31

═══════════ **Picture Puzzles** ═══════════

Puzzle Hunt 32
Socks the Same 33
Mutt Match 34
Twin Frogs 35
Crack the Code #1 36
Crack the Code #2 37
Crack the Code #3 38
Crack the Code #4 39
Test Your Memory #1 40–41
Test Your Memory #2 42–43
Test Your Memory #3 44–45
Test Your Memory #4 46–47
What's In the Toy Store? 48–49
What's In the Kitchen? 50–51

I'm Through! What Can I Do? Gr. 3–4
© The Learning Works, Inc.

Contents

(continued)

Critical Thinking

What's In – What's Out 52
More What's In – What's Out 53
Odd Word Out 54
More Odd Word Out 55
The Name Game 56
The Store Game 57
Sidney's Snakes 58
Grozzies Galore 59
Where's Wanda? 60–61
The Perfect Pet 62–63
Clowning Around 64–65
Catch a Creature 66–67

Creative Thinking

Design a Door 68
The Super Sundae 69
The World's Greatest Bubblegum 70
Create a Creature 71
Design Time 72
Create a Logo 73
Build a Robot 74–75
Create a Holiday 76
Fun Fours 77
Strain Your Brain 78
More Strain Your Brain 79

Just for Fun

Step-by-Step Pets 80
Step-by-Step Vehicles 81
Step-by-Step Sports 82
Step-by-Step Reptiles 83
Whale Grid 84
Rhino Grid 85
Sports Car Grid 86
Goldfish Grid 87
Finish the Butterfly 88
Finish the Clown 89
To the Rescue 90
Meal Maze 91

Answer Key 92–96

To the Teacher

The activities in this book are the perfect solution for kids who finish class assignments early and ask, "I'm through! What can I do?" They are ideal for extra credit and homework assignments as well as learning center activities. They can also be used to fill those extra minutes of transition time during the school day.

The book is packed with puzzles, brainteasers, pictures to draw, and mazes. It includes the following sections:

- Fun with Words
- Number and Shape Puzzles
- Picture Puzzles
- Critical Thinking
- Creative Thinking
- Just for Fun

The activities are creative, challenging, and fun! Best of all, they can be done independently by students. This makes them perfect for those times when you're busy with a reading group or working with other students. The activities and puzzles can also be used as rewards and incentives.

The activities correlate to the curriculum and cover reading, vocabulary, writing, math, and more. These ready-to-use puzzles are just what you as a busy teacher need to keep your students challenged and your classroom humming.

5

Name _____

Mystery Message #1

If you follow the directions correctly, a mystery message will appear. Read the message going across from bottom to top. Write the message on the lines below.

OCCUR	HAPPILY	BASKET	HASTILY
ONE	FLORIDA	CUPCAKE	PINK
BEET	IN	ORANGE	TENT
MICHAEL	SHAKE	SEEM	EGGS
PEANUT	PURPLE	YOUR	DOOR
ALL	SOONER	QUICKLY	WITHIN
THICK	AIRPLANE	PAUL	PUT
WEAKLY	DON'T	THAT	AWAY

- Cross off all words that begin and end with the letter T.
- Cross off all words that have exactly five letters.
- Cross off all words that are the names of colors.
- Cross off all words that are adverbs.
- Cross off all words that are proper nouns.
- Cross off all the compound words.
- Cross off all words that have two of the same vowels together.

Mystery Message

_____

_____

On the back of your paper, describe what
this message means in your own words.

Name _____

Mystery Message #2

If you follow the directions correctly, a mystery message will appear. Read the message going across from top to bottom. Write the message on the lines below.

YOU	WHILE	TWELVE	BUBBLE
KANGAROO	LETTER	BRIGHT	THE
CAT	INTERVIEW	MELLOW	IS
WON'T	BELLOW	SHE	AWAY
YELLOW	BREAD	THE	EXAMPLE
FORTY	MICE	BRUSH	WASN'T
OUR	PIZZA	WILL	FIVE
PLAY	CAN'T	US	BRANCH

- Cross off all words that are contractions.
- Cross off all words that have double consonants in the middle.
- Cross off all words that rhyme with the word *fellow*.
- Cross off all the number words.
- Cross off all words that have three syllables.
- Cross off all words that begin with the *br* blend.
- Cross off all words that are pronouns.

Mystery Message

_____

_____

On the back of your paper, describe what this message means in your own words.

Mystery Message #3

If you follow the directions correctly, a mystery message will appear. Read the message going down from top to bottom starting in the upper left. Write the message on the lines below.

VANILLA	FRIEND	WE'RE	WE
BUTTONS	EARLY	STRAWS	THE
THE	CHOCOLATE	CANADA	NIECE
I	HASN'T	CATCHES	BROOK
TOOK	STRAWBERRY	BAGELS	WORM
THEY	GEORGE	FIELD	WHO'S
CHERRY	BIRD	LOOK	HER

- Cross off all words that are pronouns.
- Cross off all words that have an *ie* spelling.
- Cross off all words that name ice cream flavors.
- Cross off all the things that have holes.
- Cross off all words that are contractions.
- Cross off all the proper nouns.
- Cross off all the compound words.
- Cross off all words that rhyme with *book*.

Mystery Message

_____

_____

On the back of your paper, describe what this message means in your own words.

Name _____

Mystery Message #4

If you follow the directions correctly, a mystery message will appear. Read the message going down from top to bottom starting in the upper left. Write the message on the lines below.

LOCATION	LEVEL	GAME	WHITE
CENT	COUNT	YOUR	BEFORE
AGREE	BROWN	RECOGNIZE	OWE
NAME	TREAT	CHICKENS	THEY'RE
ABOUT	IGLOO	ABSENT	DEPEND
DON'T	NOON	GOING	HATCHED
RED	TELEPHONE	SENT	ABOARD

- Cross off all words that begin and end with vowels.
- Cross off all words that have exactly three syllables.
- Cross off all words that rhyme with the word *same.*
- Cross off all words that name a color.
- Cross off all words that are homophones for the word *scent.*
- Cross off all words that begin and end with the same consonant.
- Cross off all words that begin with the first two letters of the alphabet.

Mystery Message

_____

_____

On the back of your paper, describe what this message means in your own words.

I'm Through! What Can I Do? Gr. 3–4
© The Learning Works, Inc.

Name _____

Ferris Wheel Fun

How many words of three or more letters can you make by moving from one connected circle to another in any direction? (Example: TEA is allowed, but TAG is not.) You may not use a letter twice in a row, but plurals are allowed. Write the words on the lines below. You can use the back of the paper if you need more room. Note: There are more than 50 words!

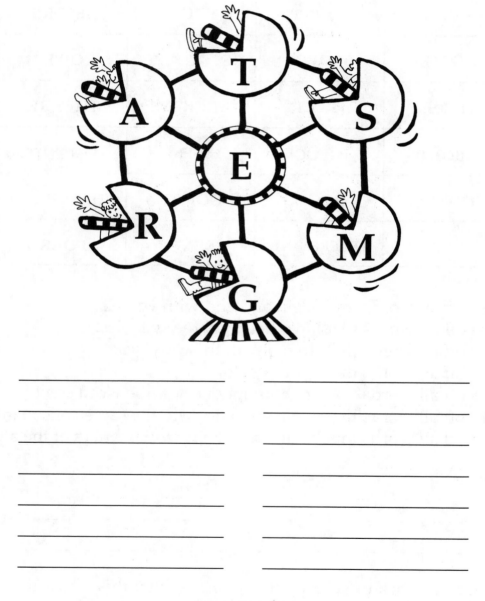

_____   _____

_____   _____

_____   _____

_____   _____

_____   _____

_____   _____

Just for Fun

Write your answers in alphabetical order on a separate piece of paper.

Name _____

Flower Power

How many words of three or more letters can you make by moving from one touching or connecting petal to another in any direction? (Example: LAST is allowed, but BET is not.) You may not use a letter twice in a row, but plurals are allowed. Write the words on the lines below. You can use the back of the paper if you need more room. Note: There are more than 50 words!

_____   _____

_____   _____

_____   _____

_____   _____

_____   _____

Just for Fun

Write your answers in alphabetical order on a separate piece of paper.

Letter Links

How many words of three or more letters can you make by moving one square at a time in any direction? You may not use a letter twice in a row, but plurals are allowed. Write the words on the lines below. Use the back of this paper if you need more room. Note: There are more than 60 words!

S	P	O	T
H	A	N	G
Y	I	R	E

_____   _____
_____   _____
_____   _____
_____   _____
_____   _____
_____   _____
_____   _____
_____   _____
_____   _____
_____   _____

Just for Fun
Make up a Letter Links puzzle for a friend to solve.

Name _____

More Letter Links

How many words of three or more letters can you make by moving one square at a time in any direction? You may not use a letter twice in a row, but plurals are allowed. Write the words on the lines below. Use the back of this paper if you need more room. Note: There are more than 100 words!

M	U	C	H
E	S	T	A
N	O	R	I
B	D	Y	P

Just for Fun
Make up a Letter Links puzzle for a friend to solve.

13

Name _____

Homophone Crossword Puzzle

Homophones are words that sound alike but have different spellings and meanings, such as *blue* and *blew*. Solve the crossword puzzle by filling in a homophone for each clue.

Across

1. serial
3. steak
4. night
7. plane
8. lone
10. peace
11. leek

Down

2. lain
3. stare
4. need
5. steal
6. grown
7. pale
9. eight

Just for Fun

Can you think of more pairs of homophones?
List them on the back of your paper.

Name _____

Synonym Crossword Puzzle

Synonyms are words that mean the same thing,
such as *happy* and *glad*. Solve the crossword puzzle
by filling in a synonym for each clue.

Across

2. instruct
3. purchase
4. vanish
9. small
10. shiver

Down

1. vacant
3. mix
5. late
6. piece
7. quick
8. ill

Just for Fun

Can you think of more pairs
of synonyms? List them on
the back of your paper.

I'm Through! What Can I Do? Gr. 3–4
© The Learning Works, Inc.

Name _____

Antonym Crossword Puzzle

Antonyms are words that mean the opposite,
such as *hot* and *cold.* Solve the crossword puzzle
by filling in an antonym for each clue.

Across

2. remember
4. finish
6. difficult
7. dirty
10. bad
12. smooth

Down

1. quiet
3. late
5. different
8. dark
9. old
11. close

Just for Fun

Can you think of more pairs of antonyms?
List them on the back of your paper.

Name _____

Hide Four

Each of these three-letter words can be found in four or more longer words. For example, *pea* is found in *speak*, *peanut*, *peaks*, and *repeat*. List the longer words under each three-letter word. If you need more room, use the back of your paper.

are

_____
_____
_____
_____
_____
_____
_____

her

_____
_____
_____
_____
_____
_____
_____

sea

_____
_____
_____
_____
_____
_____

ear

_____
_____
_____
_____
_____
_____

Just for Fun

Make up a "Hide Four" puzzle for a classmate
to solve using other three-letter words.

I'm Through! What Can I Do? Gr. 3–4
© The Learning Works, Inc.

Name _____

Noun Packages

A *noun* is a word that names a person, place, or thing. The packages below are filled with words that are nouns, but only two contain the exact same words. Find and color the bows of the two packages that contain the same nouns.

1.
toy
scooter
dad
book
candy
alligator
mouse
school

2.
alligator
school
toy
dad
candy
scooter
mouse
cloud

3.
scooter
alligator
book
cloud
candy
dad
school
mouse

4.
school
candy
book
cloud
toy
mouse
scooter
alligator

5.
cloud
dad
candy
school
toy
alligator
scooter
mouse

6.
book
toy
dad
scooter
candy
alligator
school
cloud

Name _____

Circus Sums

Find the sums. Use the answers and connect the dots in order.
You'll find something that can be found in a circus.

1. $\begin{array}{r} 87 \\ + 63 \\ \hline \end{array}$	**2.** $\begin{array}{r} 74 \\ + 36 \\ \hline \end{array}$	**3.** $\begin{array}{r} 55 \\ + 27 \\ \hline \end{array}$	**4.** $\begin{array}{r} 38 \\ + 59 \\ \hline \end{array}$
5. $\begin{array}{r} 128 \\ + 16 \\ \hline \end{array}$	**6.** $\begin{array}{r} 365 \\ + 45 \\ \hline \end{array}$	**7.** $\begin{array}{r} 440 \\ + 62 \\ \hline \end{array}$	**8.** $\begin{array}{r} 257 \\ + 88 \\ \hline \end{array}$
9. $\begin{array}{r} 453 \\ + 128 \\ \hline \end{array}$	**10.** $\begin{array}{r} 579 \\ + 334 \\ \hline \end{array}$	**11.** $\begin{array}{r} 286 \\ + 453 \\ \hline \end{array}$	**12.** $\begin{array}{r} 717 \\ + 105 \\ \hline \end{array}$
13. $\begin{array}{r} 237 \\ + 156 \\ \hline \end{array}$	**14.** $\begin{array}{r} 548 \\ + 109 \\ \hline \end{array}$	**15.** $\begin{array}{r} 607 \\ + 284 \\ \hline \end{array}$	**16.** $\begin{array}{r} 416 \\ + 198 \\ \hline \end{array}$

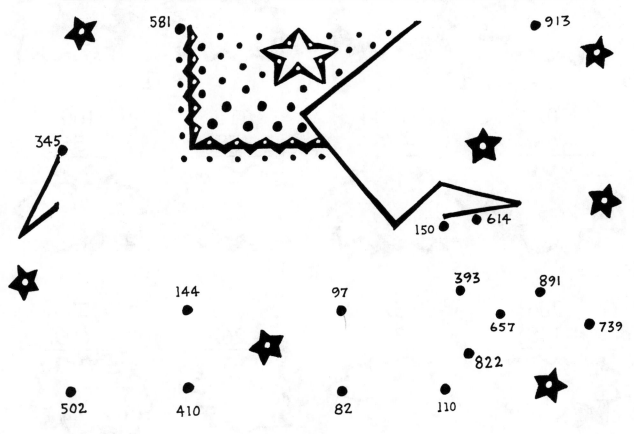

I'm Through! What Can I Do? Gr. 3–4
© The Learning Works, Inc.

Name _____

Find Four Foxes

Four foxes are hiding behind the bushes that have answers of 44.
Find the differences, and color the bushes where the four foxes are hiding.

1.
$$\begin{array}{r} 75 \\ -\ 36 \\ \hline \end{array}$$

2.
$$\begin{array}{r} 51 \\ -\ 27 \\ \hline \end{array}$$

3.
$$\begin{array}{r} 90 \\ -\ 33 \\ \hline \end{array}$$

4.
$$\begin{array}{r} 72 \\ -\ 34 \\ \hline \end{array}$$

5.
$$\begin{array}{r} 56 \\ -\ 18 \\ \hline \end{array}$$
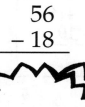

6.
$$\begin{array}{r} 67 \\ -\ 49 \\ \hline \end{array}$$

7.
$$\begin{array}{r} 93 \\ -\ 49 \\ \hline \end{array}$$

8.
$$\begin{array}{r} 85 \\ -\ 27 \\ \hline \end{array}$$

9.
$$\begin{array}{r} 107 \\ -\ 68 \\ \hline \end{array}$$

10.
$$\begin{array}{r} 120 \\ -\ 76 \\ \hline \end{array}$$
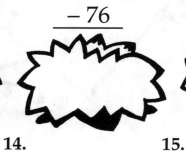

11.
$$\begin{array}{r} 111 \\ -\ 78 \\ \hline \end{array}$$

12.
$$\begin{array}{r} 100 \\ -\ 56 \\ \hline \end{array}$$

13.
$$\begin{array}{r} 206 \\ -\ 148 \\ \hline \end{array}$$
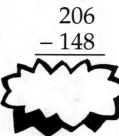

14.
$$\begin{array}{r} 574 \\ -\ 309 \\ \hline \end{array}$$

15.
$$\begin{array}{r} 311 \\ -\ 267 \\ \hline \end{array}$$

16.
$$\begin{array}{r} 798 \\ -\ 699 \\ \hline \end{array}$$

Name _____

Magic Square

Solve the magic square puzzle by placing
the numbers 1 through 9 in the boxes below
so that each row adds up to 15 going up, down, across,
and diagonally. You can only use each number one time.

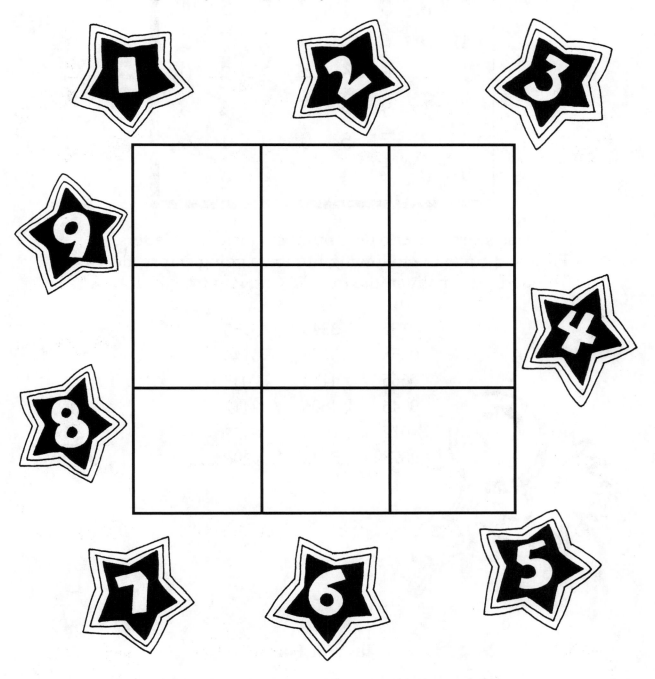

I'm Through! What Can I Do? Gr. 3–4
© The Learning Works, Inc.

Name _____

Number Search Puzzle #1

6	1	4	6	0	3	5	8
9	3	7	8	4	1	2	5
5	8	3	1	7	6	8	4
4	9	6	3	0	7	7	5
1	7	5	6	4	2	8	0
7	1	9	3	5	8	4	6
3	2	7	5	0	9	4	6
9	0	8	4	3	2	6	5

This search puzzle uses numbers instead of letters.
Find and circle the following numbers going across, down,
and diagonally in the puzzle. Can you find all 18?

0185	3348	5953
0358	3784	6146
0665	4173	7045
0946	4506	8412
1672	4736	8432
2878	5846	9296

Just for Fun

Make up a Number Search Puzzle for a friend to solve.

Name _____

Number Search Puzzle #2

8	2	7	6	4	3	0	1	2	9
4	6	0	9	2	3	1	5	8	7
5	8	3	2	1	0	7	6	9	4
3	9	6	4	5	2	8	1	7	0
0	2	1	9	3	7	5	4	6	8
9	7	5	0	1	4	3	8	6	2
2	8	4	6	7	1	5	0	3	9
5	2	3	9	8	0	4	1	7	6
1	8	7	8	6	5	0	4	2	3
7	1	3	6	4	2	9	5	8	0

This search puzzle uses numbers instead of letters.
Find and circle the following numbers going across, down,
and diagonally in the puzzle. Can you find all 24?

0129	2897	5317	7136
0145	3256	5910	7408
1258	3881	6372	7828
1413	4105	6430	8296
2276	4295	6504	8535
2315	4609	7036	9262

Just for Fun

Make up a Number Search Puzzle for a friend to solve.

Name _____

Pattern Puzzle #1

In each row, figure out the pattern of the number sequence, and write the missing number in the box. The first one has been done for you.

1.	5	10	15	20	25	30	35
2.	3	6	12	24		96	192
3.	60	58	56	54		50	48
4.	12	14	16	18		22	24
5.	34	37	40	43		49	52
6.	11	16	21	26		36	41
7.	18	20	15	17		14	9
8.	9	12	11	14		16	15

Just for Fun

Make up six Pattern Puzzles for a friend to solve.

Name _____

Pattern Puzzle #2

In each row, figure out the pattern of the number sequence, and write the missing number in the box. The first one has been done for you.

1.	2	4	7	11	16	22	29
2.	55	49	43	37		25	19
3.	8	15	10	17		19	14
4.	3	9	27	81		729	2187
5.	1	11	3	13		15	7
6.	4	9	15	22		39	49
7.	60	53	46	39		25	18
8.	26	18	27	19		20	29

Just for Fun

Make up six Pattern Puzzles for a friend to solve.

Name _____

Addition Magician

Find the sums. Use the color key to color the hidden picture.

12 = red	24 = yellow
36 = brown	18 = blue
48 = orange	

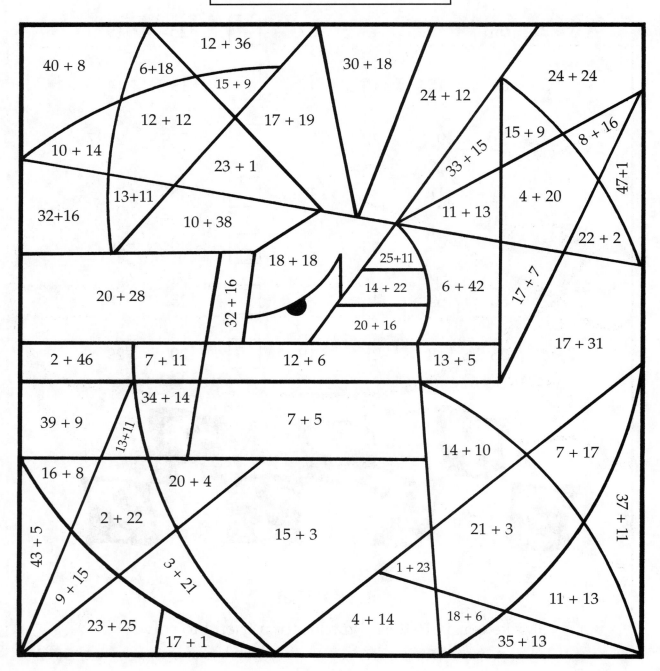

Name _____

Subtraction Submarine

Find the differences. Use the color key to color the hidden picture.

Even numbers less than 20 = green
Even numbers greater than 20 = blue
Odd numbers less than 30 = red
Odd numbers greater than 30 = brown

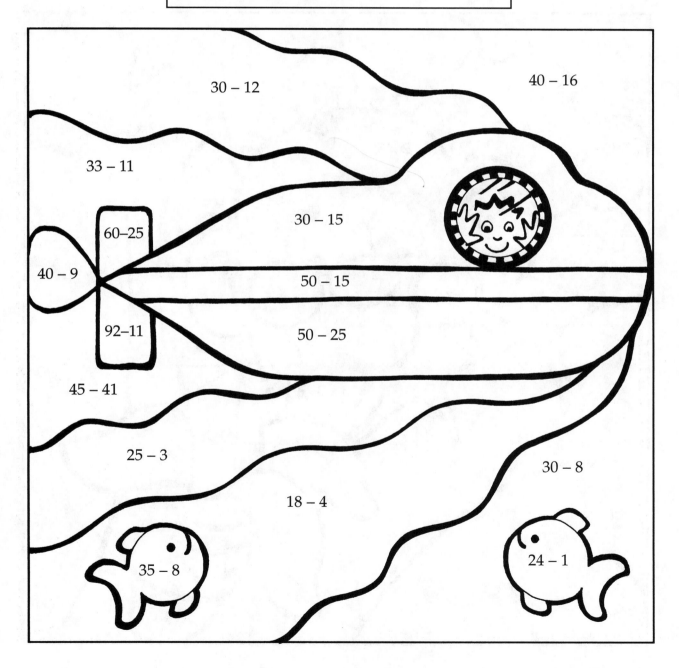

30 – 12

40 – 16

33 – 11

30 – 15

60–25

40 – 9

50 – 15

92–11

50 – 25

45 – 41

25 – 3

30 – 8

18 – 4

35 – 8

24 – 1

I'm Through! What Can I Do? Gr. 3–4
© The Learning Works, Inc.

Name _____

Multiplication Monkey

Solve each problem below. Use the color key to color the picture.

9 = orange	24 = green
10 = brown	36 = blue
12 = red	48 = yellow

Name _____

Division Dive

Solve each problem below. Use the color key to color the picture.

2 = green	6 = red
3 = brown	7 = orange
4 = blue	12 = yellow

14 ÷ 7

36 ÷ 9

21 ÷ 3

12 ÷ 2

20 ÷ 5

18 ÷ 9

12 ÷ 6

32 ÷ 8

9 ÷ 3

4 ÷ 2

24 ÷ 2

12 ÷ 4

10 ÷ 5

Name _____

Farmer Frank

Farmer Frank wanted to plant five rows of apple trees with four trees in each row. He wrote to a seed company and ordered twenty apple seeds. When his package arrived, he discovered that the seed company had made a mistake. Instead of getting twenty apple seeds, he only received ten!

But Farmer Frank was very smart. He found a way to plant the ten apple seeds in five rows with four seeds in each row. How did he do it? Draw your answer in the box below.

Note: This is not a trick question. He did not order more seeds or cut the seeds in half.

Name _____

Switch-a-Roo

Cut out the ten balls at the bottom of the page, and arrange them as shown.

Play switch-a-roo by moving exactly three balls to make the triangle

point up △ instead of down. ▽

Fill in the answers to this brain teaser puzzle.

I moved ball #_____ next to ball #_____ .

I moved ball #_____ next to ball #_____ .

I moved ball #_____ in front of ball #_____ and ball #_____ .

I'm Through! What Can I Do? Gr. 3–4
© The Learning Works, Inc.

Name _____

Puzzle Hunt

In each row, color the two puzzle pieces that are exactly alike.

1A	1B	1C	1D	1E
2A	2B	2C	2D	2E
3A	3B	3C	3D	3E
4A	4B	4C	4D	4E
5A	5B	5C	5D	5E
6A	6B	6C	6D	6E

Name _____

Socks the Same

In each row, color the two socks that are exactly alike.

I'm Through! What Can I Do? Gr. 3–4
© The Learning Works, Inc.

Name _____

Mutt Match

Find the ten matching pairs of dogs. Write their names on the lines.

Moby	Chip	Fiji	Nick
Pogo	Hash	Coco	Jake
Bear	Abby	Sage	Bud
Gus	Hank	Tex	Kelp
Lark	Tico	Zeke	Clem

_____ and _____   _____ and _____

_____ and _____   _____ and _____

_____ and _____   _____ and _____

_____ and _____   _____ and _____

_____ and _____   _____ and _____

Name _____

Twin Frogs

Find the twin frogs. Color them and write their names on the lines.

Moe	Bow	Joe	Poe	Zoe
May	Ray	Kay	Jay	Fay
Max	Jax	Pax	Bax	Dax
Ed	Ned	Fred	Jed	Red
Molly	Polly	Nolly	Jolly	Solly

The twins are _____ and _____ .

I'm Through! What Can I Do? Gr. 3–4
© The Learning Works, Inc.

Name _____

Crack the Code #1

Use the picture code to find the answer to the riddle by
writing the letters for picture symbols on the lines.
The first one has been done for you.

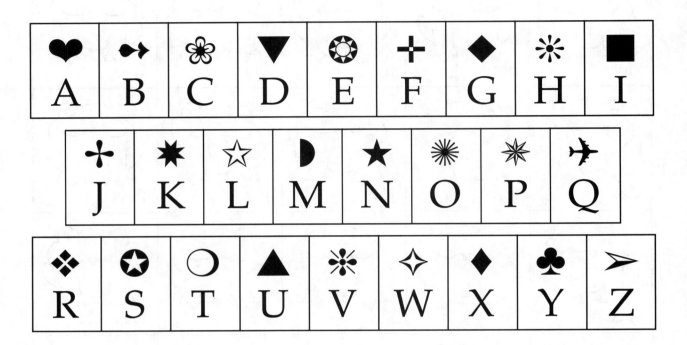

What did one earthquake say to the other?

Just for Fun

Use the picture code to send a secret message to a friend.

Name _____

Crack the Code #2

Use the picture code to find the answer to the riddle by
writing the letters for picture symbols on the lines.
The first one has been done for you.

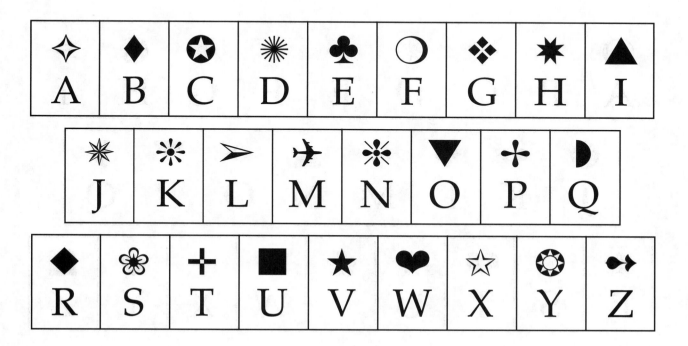

Why was the clock sad?

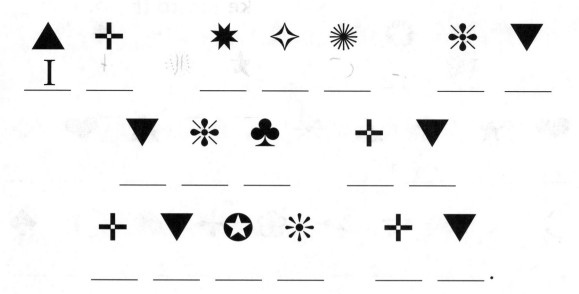

I'm Through! What Can I Do? Gr. 3–4
© The Learning Works, Inc.

Name _____

Crack the Code #3

Use the picture code to find the answer to the riddle by
writing the letters for picture symbols on the lines.
The first one has been done for you.

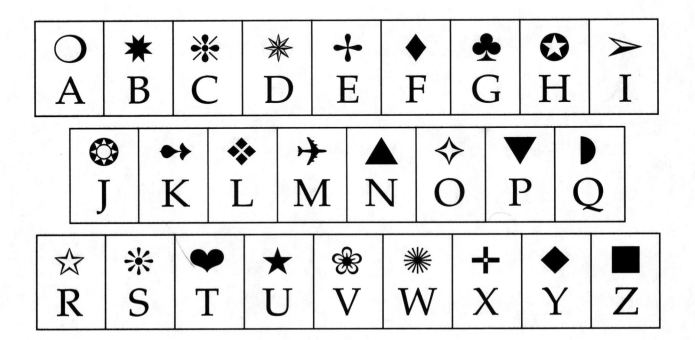

When is a car not a car?

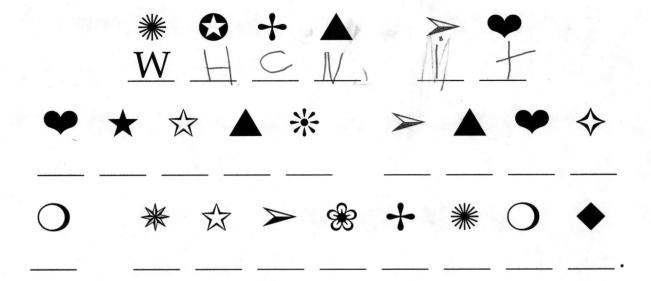

W H C N > +

Name _____

Crack the Code #4

Use the picture code to find the answer to the riddle by
writing the letters for picture symbols on the lines.
The first one has been done for you.

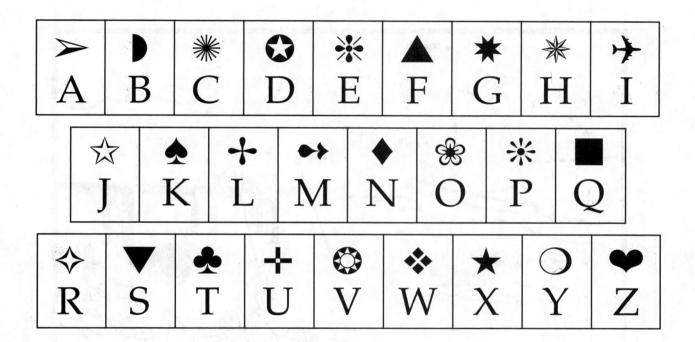

Why did the bank robber take a bath?

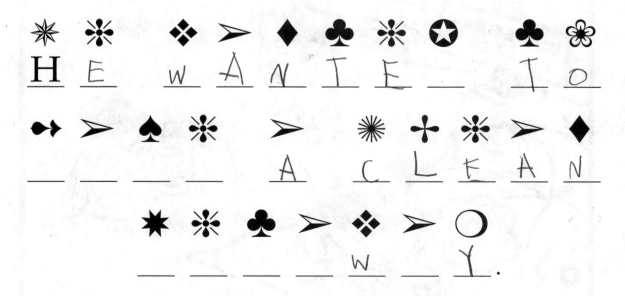

H E _ W A N T E _ T O

_ _ _ _ _ A _ C L E A N

_ _ _ _ _ W _ Y .

I'm Through! What Can I Do? Gr. 3–4
© The Learning Works, Inc.

Name _____

Test Your Memory #1

Look carefully at this picture for one minute. Try to remember as many details as possible. Then look at page 41, and see how many of the questions you can answer.

Name _____

Test Your Memory #1

1. Was a boy or a girl building the sand castle? _____

2. How many people were fishing off the pier? _____

3. What was the name of the beach? _____

4. How many people were in the ocean? _____

5. What was sitting on the post?_____

6. What game were the two boys playing? _____

7. What design was on the umbrella? _____

8. Was a man or a woman listening to the radio? _____

9. What kind of boat was in the water?_____

10. How many dogs were at the beach? _____

I'm Through! What Can I Do? Gr. 3–4
© The Learning Works, Inc.

Name _____

Test Your Memory #2

Look carefully at this picture for one minute. Try to remember as many details as possible. Then look at page 43, and see how many of the questions you can answer.

Name _____

Test Your Memory #2

1. What instrument does the person play? _____

2. What kind of beds were in the room? _____

3. How many windows were in the room? _____

4. A poster of what singer was on the wall?_____

5. Was it morning or night?_____

6. What kind of pet was in the bedroom?_____

7. How many books were on the desk?_____

8. Was there a mirror in the room?_____

9. What design was on the bedspread? _____

10. What month was it? _____

I'm Through! What Can I Do? Gr. 3–4
© The Learning Works, Inc.

Name _____

Test Your Memory #3

Look carefully at this picture for one minute. Try to remember as many details as possible. Then look at page 45, and see how many of the questions you can answer.

Name _____

Test Your Memory #3

1. How many clowns were under the big top? _____

2. How many lions were there? _____

3. What was the name of the circus? _____

4. What did the elephant have on its head? _____

5. How many people were on the high wire? _____

6. What pattern was on the clowns' costumes? _____

7. Was the person on the stilts a man or a woman? _____

8. What was the ringmaster holding in his left hand? _____

9. The girl riding the elephant had on what kind of costume? _____

10. What kind of vehicles were the clowns riding? _____

I'm Through! What Can I Do? Gr. 3–4
© The Learning Works, Inc.

Test Your Memory #4

Look carefully at this picture for one minute. Try to remember as many details as possible. Then look at page 47, and see how many of the questions you can answer.

Name _____

Test Your Memory #4

1. What time of the day was it? _____

2. What was the name of the leather store?_____

3. What was the name of the bank? _____

4. What was playing at the movie theater? _____

5. What was the sale price of the leather jacket? _____

6. What kind of dog was walking on the sidewalk? _____

7. The sign in the bookstore window announced that an author was coming to sign books on the weekend. What author was it? _____

8. How much was the lunch special at Joe's Cafe? _____

9. The taxicab was from which company? _____

10. What was in the sky? _____

11. What was the little girl wearing? _____

12. Who was riding the bicycle? _____

I'm Through! What Can I Do? Gr. 3–4
© The Learning Works, Inc.

Name _____

What's In the Toy Store?

Without looking at the checklist on page 49, carefully study this picture for one minute. Then hide this page, and use the list to check off the things you remember seeing. Caution: There are six things on the list that are not in the toy store!

Name _____

What's In the Toy Store?

After studying the toy store picture on page 48 for one minute, hide that page or turn it over. Then use this list to check off all the things that you remember seeing. Think carefully: There are six things on this list that are not in the toy store!

☐ crayons	☐ model airplane kit
☐ train	☐ fingerpaints
☐ doll	☐ bag of marbles
☐ kite	☐ coloring book
☐ stuffed animal	☐ watercolor paints
☐ beach ball	☐ toy car
☐ pick-up sticks	☐ soccer ball
☐ board game	☐ checkers
☐ drum	☐ football

I'm Through! What Can I Do? Gr. 3–4
© The Learning Works, Inc.

Name _____

What's In the Kitchen?

Without looking at the checklist on page 51, carefully study this picture for one minute. Then hide this page, and use the list to check off the things you remember seeing. Caution: There are things on the list that are not in the kitchen!

Name _____

What's In the Kitchen?

After studying the kitchen picture on page 50 for one minute, hide that page or turn it over. Then use this list to check off all the things that you remember seeing. Think carefully: There are five things on this list that are not in the kitchen!

☐ clock   ☐ pot

☐ toaster   ☐ cat

☐ salad bowl   ☐ child's drawing

☐ knife   ☐ refrigerator

☐ bananas   ☐ stove

☐ dog   ☐ stools

☐ milk carton   ☐ canisters

☐ woman   ☐ plant

☐ blender   ☐ oranges

☐ rug   ☐ pot holder

I'm Through! What Can I Do? Gr. 3–4
© The Learning Works, Inc.

Name _____

What's In – What's Out

The words in the "what's in" column all have something in common. The words in the "what's out" column do not fit in the first group of words. Decide what the words in the first group have in common, and write the answer on the line.

What's In   **What's Out**

1. pear, apple, peach   carrot, bread, lettuce

   _____

2. poodle, beagle, terrier   bark, tail, fur

   _____

3. sun, banana, butter   grape, beef, tomato

   _____

4. sandals, slippers, boots   bracelet, hat, shirt

   _____

5. Boston, Miami, Dallas   Europe, California, China

   _____

6. snow, rain, hail   ocean, fish, moon

   _____

Just for Fun

Add two or more words to the "what's in" list.

Name _____

More What's In – What's Out

The words in the "what's in" column all have something in common. The words in the "what's out" column do not fit in the first group of words. Decide what the words in the first group have in common, and write the answer on the line.

What's In	**What's Out**
1. milk, juice, water	raisin, flour, pizza

_____

2. purple, orange, yellow	paint, brush, paper

_____

3. fins, scales, gills	horns, hair, skin

_____

4. September, June, April	Tuesday, calendar, Friday

_____

5. female, girl, woman	lad, boy, mister

_____

6. summer, winter, fall	March, Thursday, May

_____

Just for Fun

Add two or more words to the "what's in" list.

I'm Through! What Can I Do? Gr. 3–4
© The Learning Works, Inc.

Name _____

Odd Word Out

In each group of words, find and circle the word
that does not belong with the others.

1. a. globe
   b. ball
   c. book
   d. sun

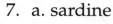
2. a. bark
   b. elm
   c. maple
   d. oak

3. a. mouse
   b. rat
   c. keyboard
   d. modem

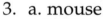
4. a. coyote
   b. horse
   c. salmon
   d. gorilla

5. a. orange
   b. daisy
   c. tulip
   d. rose

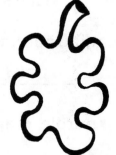

6. a. roots
   b. water
   c. leaf
   d. stem

7. a. sardine
   b. guppy
   c. shark
   d. hound

8. a. spoon
   b. couch
   c. dresser
   d. table

9. a. canoe
   b. jet
   c. kayak
   d. submarine

10. a. chicken
    b. swan
    c. deer
    d. flamingo

Just for Fun

Make up five "Odd Word Out" problems for a friend to solve.
Create an answer key so your friend can check his or her work.

Name _____

More Odd Word Out

In each group of words, find and circle the word
that does not belong with the others.

1. a. teaspoon
    b. lighthouse
    c. playground
    d. happiness

6. a. toys
    b. papers
    c. cake
    d. children

2. a. skip
    b. sad
    c. jump
    d. hop

7. a. leg
    b. eyes
    c. ears
    d. mouth

3. a. bone
    b. thank
    c. sank
    d. bank

8. a. bay
    b. river
    c. ocean
    d. island

4. a. she's
    b. well
    c. wasn't
    d. we'll

9. a. kite
    b. airplane
    c. ant
    d. bird

5. a. pair
    b. pare
    c. pear
    d. peach

10. a. huge
    b. narrow
    c. large
    d. enormous

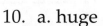

Just for Fun

Make up five "Odd Word Out" problems for a friend to solve.
Create an answer key so your friend can check his or her work.

I'm Through! What Can I Do? Gr. 3–4
© The Learning Works, Inc.

Name _____

The Name Game

Think of a word in each category that begins with the letter on the left, and fill in the chart. Give yourself one point for each correct word going across each row. You can also earn one bonus point for each row going down where you have four correct answers and no blanks.

	mammal or tree	girl's name	boy's name	insect or bird	score
B					
T					
S					
R					
bonus points					
				total points	

Name _____

The Store Game

Think of an item you would find in each store that begins with the letter on the left, and fill in the chart. Give yourself one point for each correct word going across each row. You can also earn one bonus point for each row going down where you have four correct answers and no blanks.

	clothing store	grocery store	sports store	toy store	score
P					
B					
D					
S					
bonus points					
				total points	

I'm Through! What Can I Do? Gr. 3–4
© The Learning Works, Inc.

Name _____

Sidney's Snakes

Sidney collects snakes that all have two things in common. Here are Sidney's snakes.

These snakes do not belong to Sidney. They don't have the same two things that his snakes have.

Find and color more snakes that belong to Sidney.

Just for Fun

Draw and color two more
of Sidney's snakes on the back of this paper.

Name _____

Grozzies Galore

These are Grozzies. They all have two things in common.

These are not Grozzies because they don't have the two things that Grozzies have.

Find and color other Grozzies.

Just for Fun

Draw and color two more
Grozzies on the back of this paper.

I'm Through! What Can I Do? Gr. 3–4
© The Learning Works, Inc.

Name _____

Where's Wanda?

Wanda, our superhero, has single-handedly stopped a burning meteor from crashing into Earth! Which heroine is Wanda? To find out, read each clue below. Use the clues to decide which superhero on page 61 is Wanda. Draw a circle around Wanda.

Name _____

Where's Wanda?

I'm Through! What Can I Do? Gr. 3–4
© The Learning Works, Inc.

Name _____

The Perfect Pet

The Lopez family has decided to get a new pet, but everybody has a different idea of what pet the family should buy. As you read each statement below, cross off a pet on page 63. If you do the puzzle correctly, you will find the perfect pet for the Lopez family.

Name _____

The Perfect Pet

The perfect pet for the Lopez family is the _____ .

I'm Through! What Can I Do? Gr. 3–4
© The Learning Works, Inc.

Name _____

Clowning Around

Max was just voted best clown in the circus. Your job is to figure out which clown on page 65 is Max. To find out, read each clue below. Use the clues to decide which clown is Max.

Max's costume has a fluffy, ruffled collar.

Max always wears a pointed hat with stripes on it.

Max's dark, curly hair is always sticking out of his hat.

Max has a wide smile painted on his face.

There are three large buttons on Max's costume.

There are patches sewn on each leg of Max's pants.

Max always carries a balloon wherever he goes.

Name _____

Clowning Around

1

2

3

4

5

6

7

8

Max is clown # _____ .

I'm Through! What Can I Do? Gr. 3–4
© The Learning Works, Inc.

Name _____

Catch a Creature

Help! A creature has been spotted in the neighborhood! Read each clue below. Use the clues to decide which creature on page 67 the people saw.

The creature had three sharp, pointed teeth.

The creature had five pointed toes on each foot.

The creature had scales on its arms.

The creature had a long tail with spikes.

The creature had small, beady eyes.

The creature sniffed the air with its long, black nose.

A single horn was on top of the creature's head.

Name _____

Catch a Creature

The creature the people saw is number _____ .

I'm Through! What Can I Do? Gr. 3–4
© The Learning Works, Inc.

Name _____

Design a Door

Doors come in many sizes, shapes, and styles. Doors open many different things, such as sports cars, tree houses, castles, and mansions. How many different kinds of doors can you think of? In each box below, draw and color a different door, and tell what this door opens.

Just for Fun

Which door above is your favorite? On the back of your paper, write a story about what's behind your favorite door.

Name _____

The Super Sundae

Pictured below is an ice cream sundae. Now it's up to you to add the toppings and create three different flavors of ice cream—one for each scoop.

In the box, write a description of your sundae that could be used on a menu. Make the reader's mouth water for your yummy ice cream sundae!

_____

_____

_____

_____

_____

I'm Through! What Can I Do? Gr. 3–4
© The Learning Works, Inc.

Name _____

The World's Greatest Bubblegum

Design a new type of bubblegum and give it a "catchy" name. In the space below, design the wrapper it comes in. Describe your gum's unusual flavor and what it does that no other bubblegum in the world can do.

_____
name of your bubblegum

Description of your bubblegum: _____

_____

_____

_____

_____

Just for Fun

On a separate sheet of paper, write a funny story about an unusual thing that happens to someone who chews your bubblegum.

Name _____

Create a Creature

Create a creature using any of these geometric shapes
in any size. Add other features to your creature
such as fangs, eyes, ears, teeth, hair, and a nose.

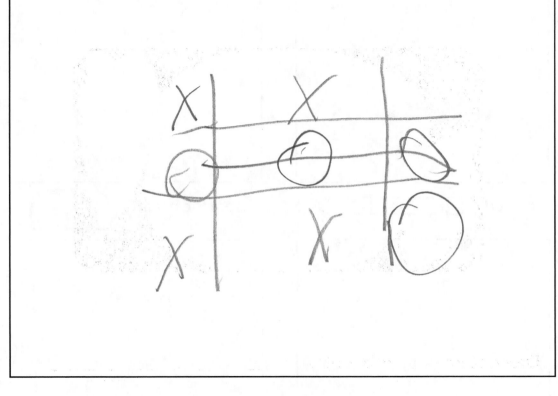

My creature's name is _____ .

It loves to eat_____ .

It is _____ feet tall and weighs _____ .

The most unusual thing about this creature is_____

_____

Just for Fun

Write a story or poem about the creature you created.

I'm Through! What Can I Do? Gr. 3–4
© The Learning Works, Inc.

Name _____

Design Time

Think about how you might change the shape of each of these items. You can expand, stretch, or modify these items in any way to make them more interesting and fun. In the spaces provided, draw pictures of your new designs.

pencil

loaf of bread

toothpaste tube

bar of soap

Just for Fun

On a separate piece of paper, create new shapes for any of the following: a computer screen, a milk carton, or a flower pot.

Name _____

 **Create a Logo**

A *logo* is a design that helps create a "look" or image for a company or business. A logo usually consists of pictures, words, and/or letters. Corporations, retail stores, restaurants, and other businesses often use logos in their advertising. Look at various logos in newspapers, magazines, and in the yellow pages of a telephone directory to get ideas. Then draw a logo for each business in the spaces provided. Give each store or business a name, and write it on the lines.

bakery

repair shop

plumber

_____

_____

_____

_____

_____

_____

sports store

restaurant

dentist

_____

_____

_____

_____

_____

_____

73

I'm Through! What Can I Do? Gr. 3–4
© The Learning Works, Inc.

Name _____

Build a Robot

Build your own personalized robot. Cut out the robot parts below. Lay them out in the box on page 75. Use as many parts as you want. When you find a design you like, paste the robot parts on your paper. Feel free to add other parts to make a one-of-a-kind robot. Then answer the questions about your robot.

Name _____

Build a Robot

robot's name: _____

robot's main job: _____

robot's best feature: _____

cost to buy robot: _____

Just for Fun

On a separate piece of paper,
write a newspaper story about your amazing robot.

I'm Through! What Can I Do? Gr. 3–4
© The Learning Works, Inc.

Create a Holiday

Create a new holiday or reason to celebrate. Here are some examples:

- Be Late for Something Day
- Eat Your Favorite Meal Day
- Iguana Appreciation Day
- Let's Not Wear Socks Day

Name your holiday or celebration. On a separate piece of paper, describe how this special day will be observed throughout the world. In your description, include foods that will be eaten, songs that will be sung, special colors that will be displayed, and other things people will do to celebrate this new holiday.

Name _____

Fun Fours

How many different ways can you write the number 4? Look at the examples below, and then add your own versions of the number 4.

4		
		4
4		
		4

I'm Through! What Can I Do? Gr. 3–4
© The Learning Works, Inc.

Name _____

Strain Your Brain

How many different uses can you think of for an ordinary, brown paper grocery bag? List your ideas below. Use the back of the paper if you need more room. You can cut the bag, color it, or add things to it. Let your ideas flow. Here are a few ideas to get you started:

hat _____ _____

vest _____ _____

_____ _____

_____ _____

_____ _____

_____ _____

_____ _____

_____ _____

_____ _____

_____ _____

Just for Fun

Choose your favorite idea
and make the project using a grocery bag.

Name _____

More Strain Your Brain

How many different uses can you think of for the plastic cubes in which some vegetables are sold in supermarkets? List your ideas below. Use the back of the paper if you need more room. You can cut the cubes, add things to them, remove pieces, or connect several cubes together. Here are a few ideas to get you started.

letter holder _____   _____

boat _____   _____

_____   _____

_____   _____

_____   _____

_____   _____

_____   _____

_____   _____

Just for Fun

Choose your favorite idea and make the project
using plastic cubes.

I'm Through! What Can I Do? Gr. 3–4
© The Learning Works, Inc.

Name _____

Step-by-Step Pets

Draw the poodle in the last box following the step-by-step pictures.

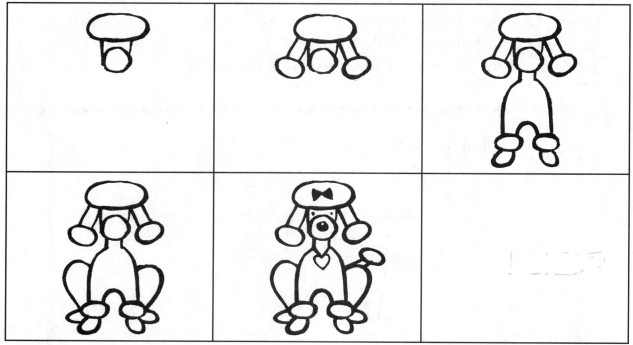

Your drawing goes here.

Draw the koala bear in the last box following the step-by-step pictures.

Your drawing goes here.

Name _____

Step-by-Step Vehicles

Draw the fire engine in the last box following the step-by-step pictures.

Your drawing goes here.

Draw the tow truck in the last box following the step-by-step pictures.

Your drawing goes here.

I'm Through! What Can I Do? Gr. 3–4
© The Learning Works, Inc.

Name _____

Step-by-Step Sports

Draw the hockey player in the last box following the step-by-step pictures.

Your drawing goes here.

Draw the basketball player in the last box following the step-by-step pictures.

Your drawing goes here.

Name _____

Step-by-Step Reptiles

Draw the turtle in the last box following the step-by-step pictures.

Your drawing goes here.

Draw the snake in the last box following the step-by-step pictures.

Your drawing goes here.

I'm Through! What Can I Do? Gr. 3–4
© The Learning Works, Inc.

Name _____

Whale Grid

To make a picture of a whale, copy the small drawings into the squares of the grid below. The numbers and letters tell you where to place each drawing. The first one has been done for you.

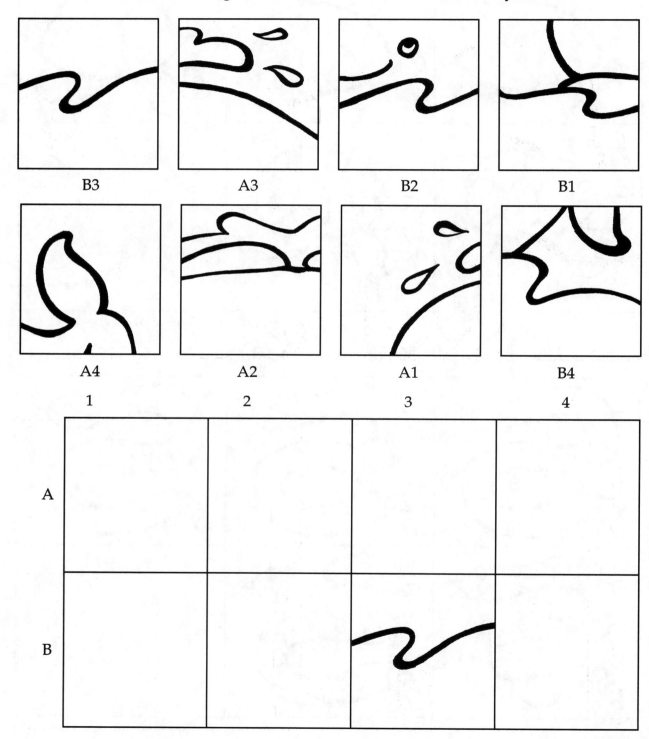

B3   A3   B2   B1

A4   A2   A1   B4

Name _____

Rhino Grid

To make a picture of a rhino, copy the small drawings into the squares of the grid below. The numbers and letters tell you where to place each drawing. The first one has been done for you.

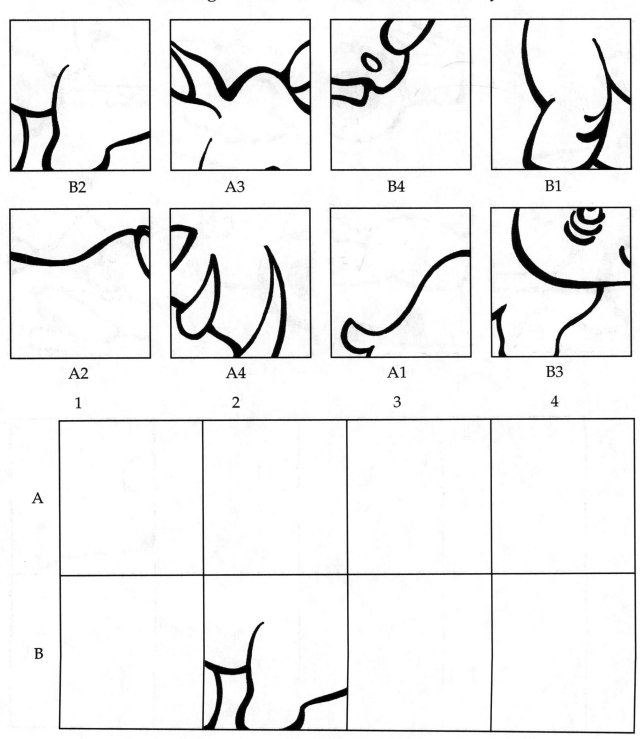

I'm Through! What Can I Do? Gr. 3–4
© The Learning Works, Inc.

Name _____

Sports Car Grid

To make a picture of a sports car, copy the small drawings into the squares of the grid below. The numbers and letters tell you where to place each drawing. The first one has been done for you.

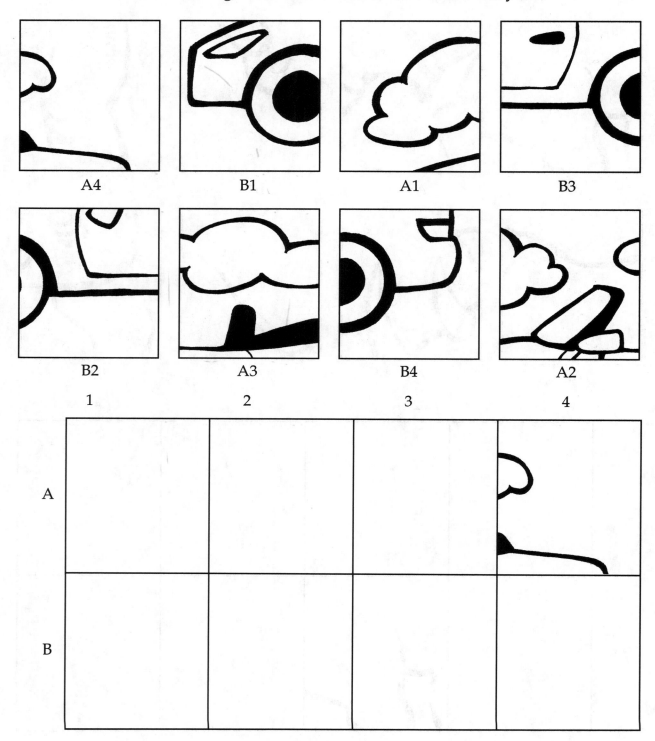

A4   B1   A1   B3

B2   A3   B4   A2

    1   2   3   4

Goldfish Grid

To make a picture of a goldfish, copy the small drawings into the squares
of the grid below. The numbers and letters tell you where to place
each drawing. The first one has been done for you.

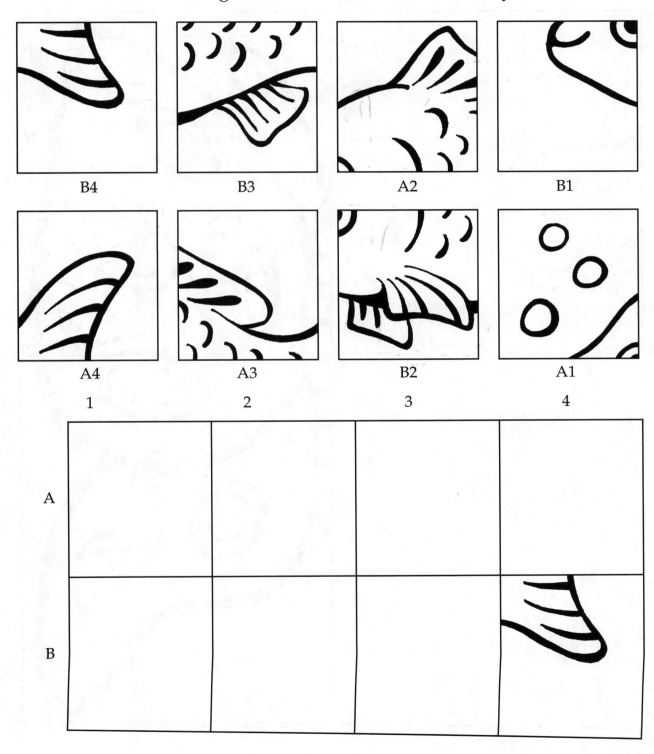

87

I'm Through! What Can I Do? Gr. 3–4
© The Learning Works, Inc.

Finish the Butterfly

Draw the other half of the butterfly to match the side
that is completed. Color your butterfly.

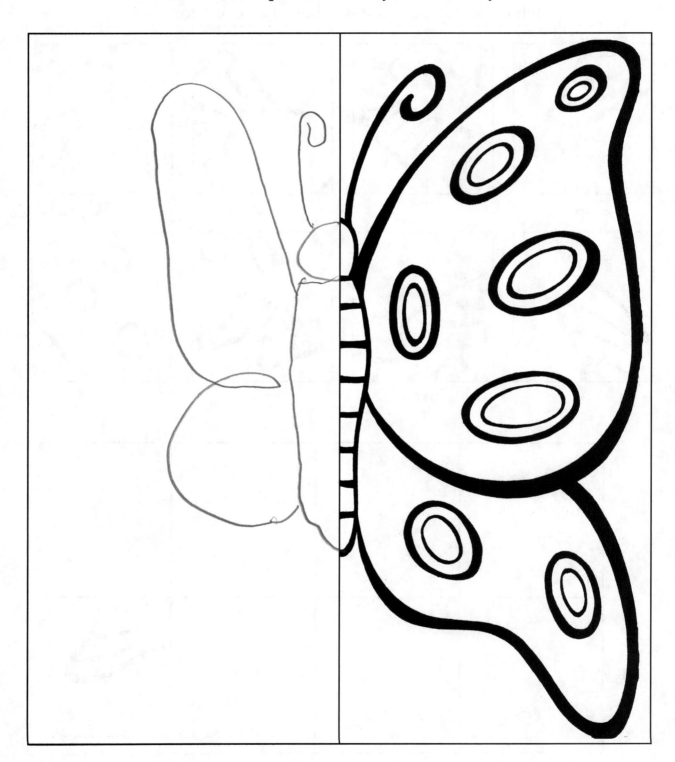

Name _____

Finish the Clown

Draw the other half of the clown to match the side
that is completed. Color your clown.

Name _____

To the Rescue

Help the fire truck get to the fire!

Name _____

Meal Maze

It's supper time! Help Fido find his way to his supper dish.

I'm Through! What Can I Do? Gr. 3–4
© The Learning Works, Inc.

Answer Key

page 6 – Mystery Message #1
Don't put all your eggs in one basket.

page 7 – Mystery Message #2
While the cat is away the mice will play.

page 8 – Mystery Message #3
The early bird catches the worm.

page 9 – Mystery Message #4
Don't count your chickens
before they're hatched.

Page 10 – Ferris Wheel Fun
Answers will vary; possible answers:

are	meat	sea
area	meats	seat
ate	mere	seats
ear	met	set
eat	rare	sets
eats	rarer	star
egret	rat	stare
egrets	rate	stares
era	rates	stem
gear	rats	stems
gem	rear	tar
gems	regret	target
get	regrets	targets
gets	rest	tea
grate	rests	tear
grates	retest	test
great	retests	tests

page 11 – Flower Power
Answers will vary; possible answers:

abstain	eats	stab
air	lab	stabs
ale	labs	stain
art	lain	stair
arts	lair	stale
bale	last	star
ban	lasts	start
bar	lean	starts
bat	least	strain
bats	nab	tab
bean	nabs	tabs
bear	rain	tale
beast	ran	tan
beasts	rat	tar
ear	rats	tart
east	sale	train
eat	sat	trial

page 12 – Letter Links
Answers will vary; possible answers:

air	oar	sang
anger	one	say
angering	onto	saying
ant	pain	share
are	paint	sharing
gone	pair	shy
grain	pairing	shying
grant	pan	shin
grasp	pang	span
grin	pant	sponge
hair	pare	spot
hang	parent	tog
hanger	paring	ton
hare	pay	tone
hay	paying	tong
hire	ran	top
hiring	rang	tops
into	range	tot
nap	ranger	yap
naps	rant	yaps
not	ring	yarn

Answer Key

page 13 – More Letter Links
Answers will vary; possible answers:

air	hardy	rip
art	harp	rob
arty	hat	rose
body	hats	roses
bone	itch	rot
bones	its	rots
botch	men	snot
boy	mend	sod
car	much	son
cars	must	sons
cat	mustard	sort
chair	nest	sorts
chairs	nests	star
char	nobody	stars
chars	nod	stone
chart	nor	stones
charts	north	story
chat	nose	such
chats	noses	tar
custard	not	tarp
cut	notary	tars
cuts	notch	toe
does	odor	toes
done	odors	ton
dose	one	tone
dot	ones	tones
dots	orator	tons
drip	orators	trait
drone	pit	trip
drones	pith	trot
dry	pits	trots
hair	pry	try
hairy	rat	use
hard	rats	

page 14 – Homophone Crossword Puzzle

Across	Down
1. cereal	2. lane
3. stake	3. stair
4. knight	4. knead
7. plain	5. steel
8. loan	6. groan
10. piece	7. pail
11. leak	9. ate

page 15 – Synonym Crossword Puzzle

Across	Down
2. teach	1. empty
3. buy	3. blend
4. disappear	5. tardy
9. tiny	6. part
10. shake	7. fast
	8. sick

page 16 – Antonym Crossword Puzzle

Across	Down
2. forget	1. noisy
4. start	3. early
6. easy	5. alike
7. clean	8. light
10. good	9. young
12. rough	11. open

page 17 – Hide Four
Answers will vary; possible answers:

are	her
arena	bother
careful	here
pare	hero
spare	there
stare	where

sea	ear
seal	earring
seam	earth
sear	hear
season	tear
seats	wear

page 18 – Noun Packages
Packages 2 and 5 have the same nouns.

page 19 – Circus Sums

1. 150	9. 581
2. 110	10. 913
3. 82	11. 739
4. 97	12. 822
5. 144	13. 393
6. 410	14. 657
7. 502	15. 891
8. 345	16. 614

Answer Key

page 20 – Find Four Foxes

1. 39
2. 24
3. 57
4. 38
5. 38
6. 18
7. **44**
8. 58
9. 39
10. **44**
11. 33
12. **44**
13. 58
14. 265
15. **44**
16. 99

Page 21 – Magic Square

4	9	2
3	5	7
8	1	6

Page 22 – Number Search Puzzle #1

Page 23 – Number Search Puzzle #2

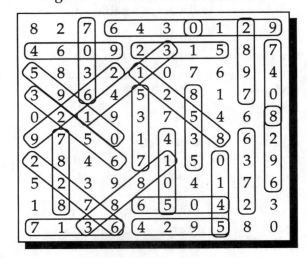

Page 24 – Pattern Puzzle #1

1. 25
2. 48
3. 52
4. 20
5. 46
6. 31
7. 12
8. 13

Page 25 – Pattern Puzzle #2

1. 16
2. 31
3. 12
4. 243
5. 5
6. 30
7. 32
8. 28

Through! What Can I Do? Gr. 3–4
Learning Works, Inc.

94

Answer Key

Page 30 – Farmer Frank
Draw a five-pointed star. Each dot stands for an apple tree planted by Farmer Frank.

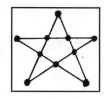

Page 31 – Switch-a-Roo
Move ball #10 next to ball #3.
Move ball #7 next to ball #2.
Move ball #1 in front of ball #8 and ball #9.

Page 32 – Puzzle Hunt
1A and 1D
2D and 2E
3A and 3C
4A and 4D
5A and 5E
6B and 6C

Page 33 – Socks the Same
1A and 1E
2B and 2C
3B and 3E
4A and 4E
5A and 5D
6B and 6C

Page 34 – Mutt Match
Moby and Tex
Chip and Kelp
Fiji and Bear
Nick and Abby
Pogo and Zeke
Hash and Clem
Coco and Lark
Jake and Hank
Sage and Tico
Bud and Gus

Page 35 – Twin Frogs
The twin frogs are Ray and Fred.

Page 36 – Crack the Code #1
It's not my fault.

Page 37 – Crack the Code #2
It had no one to tock to.

Page 38 – Crack the Code #3
When it turns into a driveway.

Page 39 – Crack the Code #4
He wanted to make a clean getaway.

Page 41 – Test Your Memory #1
1. girl
2. two
3. Butterfly Beach
4. two
5. a bird
6. catch or ball
7. flowers
8. man
9. sailboat
10. none

Page 43 – Test Your Memory #2
1. guitar
2. bunk beds
3. two
4. Elvis
5. night
6. cat
7. four
8. no
9. stars
10. April

Page 45 – Test Your Memory #3
1. two
2. three
3. Star Circus
4. a hat
5. two
6. polka dots
7. a woman
8. balloons
9. ballerina
10. tricycles

95

Answer Key

Page 47 – Test Your Memory #4

1. 5:00
2. The Leather Look
3. World Bank
4. Home Alone #28
5. $99.00
6. poodle
7. Lois Lowry
8. $6.95
9. Red Rose
10. a helicopter
11. overalls
12. a policewoman

Page 49 – What's In the Toy Store?

crayons
train
doll
stuffed animal
board game
drum
model airplane kit
bag of marbles
watercolor paints
toy car
soccer ball
checkers

Page 51 – What's In the Kitchen?

clock
toaster
salad bowl
bananas
dog
woman
blender
pot
child's drawing
refrigerator
stove
stools
canisters
plant
pot holder

Page 52 – What's In – What's Out

1. They are all fruits.
2. They are all breeds of dogs.
3. They are all yellow.
4. They are all footwear.
5. They are all cities in the United States.
6. They are all forms of weather.

Page 53 – More What's In – What's Out

1. They are all liquids you can drink.
2. They are all colors.
3. They are all parts of a fish.
4. They are all months of the year.
5. They are all synonyms for a lady.
6. They are all seasons.

page 54 – Odd Word Out

1. c. book
2. a. bark
3. b. rat
4. c. salmon
5. a. orange
6. b. water
7. d. hound
8. a. spoon
9. b. jet
10. c. deer

page 55 – More Odd Word Out

1. d. happiness
2. b. sad
3. a. bone
4. b. well
5. d. peach
6. c. cake
7. a. leg
8. d. island
9. c. ant
10. b. narrow

page 58 – Sidney's Snakes

Sidney's snakes have
forked tongues and six stripes.

page 59 – Grozzies Galore

The Grozzies are smiling
and they have two horns.

page 61 – Where's Wanda?

Wanda is number 5.

page 63 – The Perfect Pet

The perfect pet for the Lopez family is a cat.

page 65 – Clowning Around

Max is number 5.

page 67 – Catch a Creature

The creature the neighbors saw
is number 6.

Through! What Can I Do? Gr. 3–4
e Learning Works, Inc.

96